DOUGLAS MacARTHUR

An American Hero
by Barbara Silberdick Feinberg

A Book Report Biography
FRANKLIN WATTS
A Division of Grolier Publishing
New York / London / Hong Kong / Sydney
Danbury, Connecticut

Frontispiece: Five-star general, Douglas MacArthur

Cover illustration by Joan M. McEvoy

Photographs ©: AP/Wide World Photos: 24, 63, 75; Corbis-Bettmann: 10, 39, 52, 60, 69, 73, 84, 107, 108 (UPI), 26, 43, 86; Culver Pictures: 110 (ACME), 2 (Sy Seidman Collection), 35; MacArthur Memorial, Norfolk, VA. 19, 51 (MacArthur Archives), 13, 41, 46, 47, 54, 79, 88 (US Army Signal Corps), 21, 57, 116.

Visit Franklin Watts on the Internet at:
http://publishing.grolier.com

Library of Congress Cataloging-in-Publication Data
Feinberg, Barbara Silberdick.
      Douglas MacArthur: an American hero / by Barbara Silberdick
Feinberg.
            p. cm.—(A book report biography)
      Includes bibliographical references and index.
      Summary: Examines the childhood, training, and career of the man
known for his military leadership during World War II, the administration
of occupied Japan after the war, and the Korean war.
      ISBN: 0-531-11562-3 (lib. bdg.)   0-531-15950-7 (pbk.)
      1. MacArthur, Douglas, 1880–1964—Juvenile literature. 2. Gener-
als—United States—Biography—Juvenile literature. 3. United States.
Army—Biography—Juvenile literature. 4. United States—History, Military—20th century—Juvenile literature. [1. MacArthur, Douglas,
1880–1964. 2. Generals.] I. Title. II. Series.
E745.M3F45 1999
355'.0092—dc21
[B]   98-29755
                                                                                              CIP
                                                                                                AC

GROLIER
PUBLISHING

CONTENTS

CHAPTER ONE
A HISTORIC MOMENT
9

CHAPTER TWO
A SON OF THE ARMY
16

CHAPTER THREE
THE SEARCH FOR GLORY
31

CHAPTER FOUR
THE COURAGE OF HIS CONVICTIONS
49

CHAPTER FIVE
A PROMISE KEPT
67

CHAPTER SIX
THE AMERICAN WAY
83

CHAPTER SEVEN
A RISKY BUSINESS
97

CHAPTER EIGHT
AN OLD SOLDIER
112

CHRONOLOGY
117

GLOSSARY
120

A NOTE ON SOURCES
122

FOR MORE INFORMATION
124

INDEX
126

Dedicated to my uncle, Charles Silverdick, who was stationed in New Guinea during World War II.

Acknowledgments

I am grateful to Michael Neft for the loan of some excellent books on Asia; to Marianne Mosbach for suggesting two chapter titles; and to Lorna Greenberg for her superb editorial skills and for her encouragement.

Note to My Readers

Since Douglas MacArthur's grandfather, father, brother, and son were all named Arthur, I have used their names as little as possible to avoid confusion. Instead I refer to them by mentioning their relationship to the general.

CHAPTER ONE

A HISTORIC MOMENT

"I was on my own, standing on the quarterdeck with only God and my own conscience to guide me," wrote General Douglas MacArthur, Supreme Commander for Allied Powers. He had been assigned to accept the formal surrender of Japan to end World War II. With no instructions from the U.S. government, he arranged for the ceremony to take place on September 2, 1945, aboard the battleship *Missouri* in Tokyo Bay.

The *Missouri* was decorated to mark the occasion. A faded thirty-one-star American flag was displayed on one bulkhead. In 1853, that flag had crossed the Pacific Ocean with Admiral Matthew Perry, who had opened Japan to American trade. On the main mast waved the American flag that had flown over the U.S. capitol on December 7, 1941—the day Japanese forces had launched a surprise attack on the American naval base at

*Crew members fill every available space,
even gun turrets, to watch the historic scene
as the Japanese foreign minister signs the
World War II official surrender document
aboard the* U.S.S. Missouri.

Pearl Harbor, Hawaii. For the next four years, the
United States had waged war against Japan and
the other Axis powers, Germany and Italy.

On his way to the ceremonies, MacArthur
walked past battle-weary sailors in fresh white

uniforms. They lined the upper decks and g
rets, leaning over to snap pictures with the
eras. One sailor whispered to another, "
Mac. Ain't he got no ribbons?" His n
explained, "If he wore them, they'd go cle
his shoulder."

General of the Army Douglas MacArth
the highest rank in the military. He was on
most decorated soldiers in American histo:
ing been awarded twenty-two medals, in
thirteen for heroism. He wore none on th
Like the other American officers, MacArth
dressed in simple open-necked khakis. I
trast, the admirals and generals of other i
allied with the United States to defeat
wore colorful uniforms, decorated with bat
bons and medals.

The representatives of the United
Great Britain, Australia, the Netherlands,
da, China, New Zealand, France, and Russi
up around a mess table covered with a
cloth. Facing them stood eleven representat
the Japanese government: four diplomats
mal clothes and seven military officers in
drab uniforms.

The ship's chaplain opened the cerer
with a prayer. The "Star Spangled Banner" p
over a loudspeaker. Then sixty-five-year-ol
eral MacArthur spoke. He urged the victo:
the vanquished to build a world "dedicated

dignity of man and the fulfillment of his most cherished wish—for freedom, tolerance and justice." Next he asked the Japanese to sign two copies of the surrender. One was bound in leather for the Americans; the other, bound in canvas, was for the Japanese.

After they signed, MacArthur sat down and used six pens to add his name to the documents. He handed one pen each to a British and to an American general who had both spent four miserable years in Japanese prisoner of war camps. One he set aside for his wife. The remaining pens would be sent to the U.S. Military Academy at West Point, the Naval Academy at Annapolis, and the National Archives. Finally, the Allied delegates added their names to the documents. Once more, MacArthur stood before the microphone. "Let us pray," he said, "that peace be now restored to the world and that God will preserve it always. These proceedings are closed."

A COMPLEX PERSON

George C. Kenney, a member of the general's World War II staff, claimed that people either admired or disliked MacArthur. They were "never neutral." According to Gallup opinion polls, most Americans thought he was a hero. The general's troops were divided in their opinions. The men MacArthur commanded during World War I were

As Supreme Allied Commander, General Douglas MacArthur signs the surrender document. Behind MacArthur are General Jonathan Wainwright who spent four years in Japanese prisoner of war camps after surrendering Corregidor to the Japanese, and General A.E. Percival, the British commander who surrendered to the Japanese at Singapore.

proud to serve with him. They admired him for risking his life to lead them in combat. Enlisted men in World War II, however, mocked him for rarely visiting the front lines. They saw him as a stiff, demanding commander.

Politicians also differed in their judgments of him. President Harry S. Truman disliked him before they had even met. He complained in a private memo that the general was "Mr. Prima Donna, Brass Hat, Five Star MacArthur." Liberals would not forget occasions when he disregarded the civil rights of protesters and demonstrators, but they admired his efforts to bring democracy to Asia. Conservative Republicans shared most of his views on foreign affairs but not his desire to free subject peoples from colonial rulers.

"Mr. Prima Donna, Brass Hat, Five Star MacArthur."

Critics and fans alike agreed that MacArthur was self-centered and conceited. He rehearsed his speeches and comments privately, trying to make them seem spontaneous rather than prepared. Like an actor, he sought attention. His corncob pipe, battered field cap, sunglasses, and aviator jacket were his personal trademarks. They guaranteed that people would instantly recognize him. He irritated his superiors with requests for medals and promotions, but he earned them.

MacArthur was a complex person. His manners were formal, stiff, and correct. A shy man, he did not make friends easily and was uncomfortable at informal gatherings. Yet he inspired loyalty and devotion from his hardworking staff. He had a first-rate intellect and was a brilliant strategist, often outwitting the enemy. He was also a man of action, determined to succeed. Perhaps it was his upbringing that made him want to be the best, to win, to be a brave American soldier. It was probably his upbringing that also led him to irritate and defy civilian leaders. This trait finally resulted in his dismissal from command even though he was a five-star general.

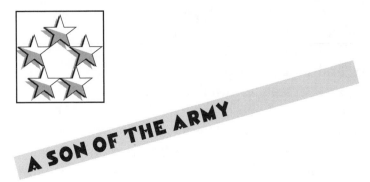

CHAPTER TWO

A SON OF THE ARMY

"Douglas MacArthur was born on January 26 [1880], while his parents were away," proclaimed Norfolk, Virginia, newspapers. MacArthur found this announcement so funny that he included it in his memoirs. His mother, of course, was present at his birth. However, he had arrived earlier than expected, before his parents could return to Norfolk from the Arsenal Barracks in Little Rock, Arkansas, to await his birth. His two older brothers, Arthur (1876) and Malcolm (1878), had been born in Norfolk, his mother's hometown.

A MILITARY COUPLE

Douglas's mother, Mary "Pinky" Pinkney Hardy, was born into an old Virginia colonial family. Her father was a wealthy cotton broker. Her ancestors served under George Washington during the

American Revolution and her brothers fought for the South in the Civil War. At a party in New Orleans during the winter of 1874, she was attracted to a former Union officer, now serving in the U.S. Army, Captain Arthur MacArthur Jr.

In May 1875, Pinky and Arthur were married. Arthur's father had been born in Scotland but raised in the United States. He had become a respected politician and federal judge in Milwaukee, Wisconsin. When the Civil War broke out, Arthur Jr. abandoned his law studies and his goal of attending West Point. He was eager to join up. Through his father's political influence, he was appointed an officer in the 24th Regiment, Wisconsin. In November 1863, the regiment helped break the Confederate line on Missionary Ridge overlooking Chattanooga, Tennessee. Under heavy enemy fire, Arthur retrieved the regimental flag, helped reunite the troops, and led them to the top of the ridge. Years later, he received a Medal of Honor, the nation's highest military decoration, for this act of heroism. He decided to stay in the army.

ON THE MOVE

As the child of a professional soldier, Douglas MacArthur could be called an army brat. He became used to moving from one military base to another when his father was transferred. Listening to bugle calls and standing at attention during flag ceremonies were a part of Douglas's daily routine. His earliest memories were of outposts in New Mexico. Troops under his father's command protected settlers and the Navahos from a few bands of marauding Indians not yet confined to reservations.

The three MacArthur boys learned to ride horses and shoot. Douglas had his own pony. He often rode off into the desert with his brother Arthur. Once they saw a lone camel, a survivor of a herd that had been brought to the United States when Franklin Pierce was president in the mid-1850s. Douglas drank in the enlisted men's colorful tales of Civil War exploits and frontier adventures. His favorite stories were of his father's heroic deeds.

Malcolm died of the measles at age five, and Pinky devoted herself to her two surviving sons. She was a strong, demanding woman who ruled the MacArthur household. "We were to do what was right, no matter what the personal sacrifice might be. . . . Two things we must never do: never lie, never tattle," Douglas wrote. She taught her sons to read and to write. She also insisted that they have good manners. Her husband loved to

"Never lie, never tattle."

*Young Douglas MacArthur (left) with his
brother Arthur and parents Major General Arthur
MacArthur Jr. and Pinky MacArthur at Fort Selden,
New Mexico, about 1885*

read and study at the end of the day. He, too, helped to educate his sons.

LESSONS TO BE LEARNED

At the age of six, in 1886, Douglas attended public school for the first time. He entered second grade at Fort Leavenworth, Kansas. Like many army children, he completed grade school in a different place—in his case in Washington, D.C. He was a poor student, easily distracted, and bored by his studies. The young MacArthur also took dancing classes in which he learned how to behave in the company of young ladies.

Pinky taught her sons to be courageous. Neither Douglas nor his brother were allowed to give up, despite disappointments or obstacles. Once, during a summer vacation in Norfolk, thirteen-year-old Douglas tried to earn spending money by selling newspapers. He returned home the first day with a stack of unsold papers. The other newsboys would not let him invade their territory. Pinky told him to go out the next day and not come home until he had sold his papers. Despite a bloody nose and a black eye, he succeeded.

In 1893, the MacArthurs moved to Houston, Texas. Douglas enrolled in the West Texas Military Academy. "There came a desire to know, a seeking for the reason why, a search for the truth," MacArthur noted. At last, he was challenged by interesting and difficult subjects, such as math, Greek, and Latin. No longer bored, Douglas earned A's in all his studies.

"A search for the truth."

At first, he did not fit in at school. He was a day student while his classmates were boarders.

Also, they were jealous of him because he had become an outstanding student.

In his third year, he earned his classmates' friendship through sports. He was not a natural athlete, but he was determined. Eventually he became a tennis champion, a football quarterback, and a baseball shortstop and bunter. He valued these achievements more than the gold medal he won for academic excellence at graduation in 1897. By then, his brother Arthur had

The undefeated 1896 West Texas Military Academy football team, on which Douglas MacArthur (foreground, with numerals) played end

graduated from the U.S. Naval Academy at Annapolis, Maryland, and was starting a career as a naval officer. Douglas set his sights on West Point.

A CADET AT WEST POINT

The children of army officers had difficulty getting appointments to the military academy because they moved around too much. Members of Congress usually sponsored boys from their own districts. Douglas's grandfather and father had anticipated this problem. Before his death in 1896, Judge MacArthur had asked some of the politicians he knew to write letters of recommendation for his grandson. Douglas's father made similar requests. These were sent first to outgoing president Grover Cleveland, then to incoming president William McKinley. Presidents could make at-large appointments to West Point, but neither chose Douglas.

The judge's crony, Congressman Theabold Otjen of Milwaukee, Wisconsin, sponsored an exam to select his candidate for West Point. He invited Douglas to come and compete. Pinky moved with Douglas to Milwaukee. She arranged for her son to spend the next year preparing for the test. Every weekend they visited Douglas's father, who had been posted to St. Paul, Minnesota.

The night before the exam, Douglas felt sick and couldn't sleep. The next morning Pinky escorted him to the test room. She told him, "Doug, you'll win if you don't lose your nerve. You must believe in yourself, my son, or no one else will believe in you." MacArthur later wrote, "It was a lesson I never forgot." He earned the highest score and won the appointment.

"You must believe in yourself."

During the brief Spanish-American War of 1898, MacArthur's father and brother were sent to fight in the Philippine Islands, a Spanish colony off the coast of Asia. Anxious to join them, Douglas wanted to postpone his admission to the military academy. His father, who as a young man had abandoned his dream of entering West Point to fight in the Civil War, refused to let his son make a similar sacrifice. Instead Douglas took and passed the stiff West Point entrance exam and became a cadet at the all-male academy.

Since her husband was away in the Philippines and she had no home of her own, Pinky decided to move into a hotel near the military academy. There she entered into a friendly competition with Mrs. Frederick N. Grant. Her son, Ulysses S. Grant III, the grandson of President Ulysses Grant, was Douglas's classmate. From

*Pinky MacArthur with Douglas at West Point in
1900, when he was a first-year cadet at the academy*

her hotel room, Pinky could see if the lights were on in Douglas's room, a sign that he was studying. She wanted him to be more successful than Ulysses S. Grant III.

Pinky monitored her son's active social life as well as his studies. She invited any young woman who especially admired him to tea. Then she would delicately explain that Douglas "was already married to his career." He did not object. That way, he could continue to meet and date many other women.

Pinky remained near her son for two years. During that time, her husband became a national hero. After the American victory over Spain, he put down a rebellion of Filipino guerrillas. They had hoped to gain independence and were angry that their country had been made an American protectorate. After being promoted to military governor of the islands, he was noted for his fairness to the Filipino people. However, Arthur MacArthur and William H. Taft, one of the civilians sent to run the government, disagreed over how to handle the remaining guerrillas. When Taft became civilian governor of the islands, MacArthur was relieved of command. Although he eventually advanced to the rank of lieutenant general, he was never again given a major command. He was bitter when he retired. Fifty years

General Arthur MacArthur Jr. (left), pictured here with the Filipino peace commissioners in a drawing for Harper's Weekly *magazine, drew public notice for ending a guerrilla rebellion, but his fame brought Douglas even more hazing.*

later, his son Douglas would also have difficulties accepting civilian control of the military.

HAZING

Hazing "plebes," or first-year cadets, was a long-standing West Point tradition. Upperclassmen made plebes fulfill ridiculous, sometimes abusive demands. This was supposed to weed out unsuitable officers. As a plebe, Douglas was singled out for abuse. Because his father had fought for the Union, southern cadets repeatedly made him stand at attention and recite his father's Civil War exploits. Other upperclassmen picked on him because of his father's growing fame in the Philippines. Often he was ordered to remain as still as a statue for an hour at a time. Once he was forced to do deep knee bends over broken glass until he fainted. Later his legs went into spasms. His courage earned him the respect of the cadet corps.

In 1900, a student died after resigning from the academy—possibly as a result of hazing. So, that same year, President McKinley demanded an official inquiry into the tradition. As a victim of particularly vicious hazing, Douglas was ordered to testify.

The hearing was awkward for him. He was asked to name those who had tormented him. He wasn't sure what to do. During a recess in the proceedings, his mother slipped him a long note reminding him never to lie and never to tattle. Douglas supplied only the names of cadets who had already admitted their guilt or who had resigned. Then he pleaded not to be dismissed from the academy even though he had failed to fully obey the order to name all the cadets involved. Perhaps because of his father's fame and connections, Douglas was not asked to leave West Point.

In January 1901, Douglas was called before a congressional committee investigating hazing at the military academy. Again he refused to identify all of his tormentors. He made his experiences seem routine when he told the lawmakers, "The hazing that I underwent was in no way more severe or more calculated to place me in a serious physical condition than has ordinarily taken place." At the end of the investigation, Congress ordered the academy to stop dangerous hazing practices.

AN OUTSTANDING CADET

Douglas's academic record won the admiration of the corps. He graduated first in his class, a position he had held for three of the four years. Aided by a phenomenal memory and ability to concentrate, he excelled in math, chemistry, and physics. Marring his almost perfect record were a few demerits—for an improper salute, an appearance out of uniform, and tardiness. Class standing was determined by both grades and demerits.

Douglas achieved another honor his last year at the academy. He was made first captain of the cadet corps, and so served as the superintendent of the academy's representative to the cadets. It was unusual for a cadet to be first captain of the corps as well as first in his class. His classmates also voted

_____

"Most likely to succeed."

_____

him most likely to succeed. They did not resent his achievements, but they did fault him for his vanity and pride.

Douglas's athletic record was not impressive. He did, however, play left field in the first Army–Navy baseball game, held at Annapolis in 1901. His team won. For the rest of his life, Douglas proudly wore West Point regulation gray bathrobes displaying his academy baseball letter. In his third year he managed the football team. He would later become its most devoted fan.

Douglas graduated from the U.S. Military Academy at West Point in June 1903 and was commissioned as a second lieutenant. He took the academy's motto, "Duty, Honor, Country," to heart. He also heeded his mother's advice to follow or even exceed his father's example. He had wanted to join the infantry, but his father disapproved. Infantry promotions were too slow in peacetime. Instead, Douglas was assigned to the Army Corps of Engineers. To his delight, he was ordered to the Philippines.

"Duty, Honor, Country."

CHAPTER THREE

THE SEARCH FOR GLORY

"I heard the bullets whistle, and believe me, there is something charming in the sound," MacArthur wrote to Pinky from the Philippines. In a search for glory, he had turned a routine engineering assignment to build docks in the city of Tacloban into an adventure. He knew that some local tribes were still hostile to Americans. Nevertheless, he led his men into the jungle to get timber. They were ambushed by two guerrillas. Their bullets pierced MacArthur's hat before he shot them.

The young officer shared his father's enthusiasm for the Philippines. He learned as much as he could about the country and its people. He also passed an exam to become a first lieutenant. Then, after a bout of malaria, he was ordered stateside.

A TOUR OF THE FAR EAST

In 1905, he joined his father on an eight-month inspection tour of military installations in the Far East. The Russo-Japanese War (1904–1905) was forcing Americans to pay attention to Asia. The MacArthurs visited Japan, Singapore, Java, Burma, India, Thailand, and China. In Thailand, Lieutenant MacArthur attended a royal dinner, and when the lights failed, he replaced a broken fuse. The king wanted to give him a medal for his prompt action. The young officer declined the honor. He had been practical, not heroic.

MacArthur drew several conclusions from his trip. First, he observed that Japan posed a growing threat to the peace of Asia. Its soldiers were disciplined and brave. Second, he reasoned that because the subject peoples of Asia distrusted their colonial rulers, Japanese expansionists could take advantage of this explosive situation. Finally, MacArthur concluded that "the future . . . of America . . . was irrevocably entwined with Asia and its island outposts." He would hold this belief for the rest of his life.

THE RELUCTANT ENGINEER

In 1906, MacArthur was assigned to advanced training at the Washington Barracks and was given special duties at the White House, which he enjoyed. As an assistant military aide, he attended receptions given by President Theodore Roosevelt. He admired the president's energy and lack of formality and was flattered when Roosevelt asked for his opinions on the Far East.

He was no longer enthusiastic about dredging rivers and harbors or building new docks. He lost interest in his training, which was noted on his record. He received another bad report after being transferred to an engineering post in Milwaukee.

From 1908 to 1911, he served at Fort Leavenworth, Kansas, and discovered that he preferred commanding men to supervising engineering projects. He was put in charge of one of the lowest rated companies on the post. MacArthur whipped them into shape by appealing to their pride. Promoted to captain, he became an instructor at the engineering school. Temporary assignments took him to Texas and Panama. The life of an army engineer, however, did not offer the action and excitement he craved.

In September 1912, his father died suddenly. MacArthur wrote, "Never have I been able to heal the wound in my heart." He carried his father's

"Never have I been able to heal the wound in my heart."

photograph for the rest of his life. Captain MacArthur moved his grieving mother to his quarters at Fort Leavenworth. He was miserable—missing his father, dissatisfied with his work, and troubled by his mother's constant complaints about their housing.

His father's friend, Chief of Staff Leonard Wood, came to his rescue. He transferred MacArthur to the Army General Staff. It supervised personnel, equipment, planning, and overall military strategy. After a year or so of routine assignments, Wood gave MacArthur a chance to undertake a dangerous and difficult mission. He sent the captain to Veracruz, Mexico, to gather military intelligence.

MISSION TO VERACRUZ

In April 1914, it looked as if the United States might go to war with Mexico. The U.S. Navy had blockaded Veracruz harbor. This action prevented a German munitions ship from delivering arms to the government of Mexican dictator Victoriano Huerta. (The United States had supported the constitutional regime Huerta had overthrown.) Then local officials had arrested a detail of marines sent ashore for supplies. The marines were soon set free, and the officials apologized. However, they refused to give a twenty-one-gun

MacArthur in Veracruz, 1914

salute to the American flag as the commanding admiral demanded. Using this insult as an excuse to intervene, President Woodrow Wilson ordered the navy to occupy Veracruz. Army reinforcements were sent to help the navy hold the city of 40,000 residents.

Arriving on May 1, MacArthur quickly discovered that Veracruz lacked horses or trucks to transport troops if war were to be declared and the army had to march inland. There were few locomotives but plenty of railroad cars. Determined to become a hero, the captain bribed several Mexican railroad workers to help him locate and seize locomotives behind enemy lines. After a brief skirmish, they stole three engines from Alvarado, forty miles away. They spent six hours fighting mounted guerrillas, with bullets whizzing overhead, on their way back to Veracruz. The captain continued to gather intelligence until he returned to Washington in September of 1915.

Wood recommended him for a Medal of Honor, but the request was denied. No army officers witnessed MacArthur's raid. Also, he had not been acting under a local commander's orders. The army did not want to encourage other staff officers to go off on their own to seek adventure. However, MacArthur was promoted to major and put to work on defense projects.

The war with Mexico was averted through the mediation of Argentina, Brazil, and Chile, and Huerta abdicated. A month later, the U.S. government faced a more serious problem than its relations with Mexico. In August 1914, World War I broke out in Europe, with Germany and Austria pitted against England, France, and Russia.

FOUNDING THE RAINBOW DIVISION

In 1916, Major MacArthur became an assistant to the secretary of war, Newton D. Baker. The secretary of war was the civilian head of the army and, at that time, a member of the president's cabinet. MacArthur was his unofficial public relations officer and was responsible for presenting the army's views to reporters.

On April 6, 1917, America entered World War I. German submarines had attacked U.S. merchant ships in the waters off Britain and in the Mediterranean Sea. The Germans wanted to prevent arms and food from reaching England and France, and they were willing to break an earlier pledge not to sink ships without warning.

Part of MacArthur's job was to help the public accept the draft, which required young men to enter military service. There weren't enough regular army officers to train the draftees. So Baker and MacArthur suggested that President Wilson call up the National Guard (state military forces) to help out. MacArthur expected the states to compete to be the first to offer their forces. He proposed that individual guard units from different states be selected, "Like a rainbow." Thus, the Rainbow (42nd) Division was born. At MacArthur's request, Baker signed his promotion to colonel and transferred him to the infantry. He left for France in October 1917 as the Rainbow Division's chief of staff.

"Like a rainbow."

Colonel MacArthur was soon waging a private war against the top American brass in France. In November, the leader of the American Expeditionary Forces, Major General John J. "Black Jack" Pershing shifted thirty-three of MacArthur's hand-picked officers to other commands, ignoring MacArthur's protests. Then Pershing decided to break up the Rainbow Division to bring other undermanned divisions up to strength. MacArthur appealed to Secretary Baker, and the Rainbow Division was saved.

A PIECE OF THE ACTION

Assigned to the French army in northeastern France, MacArthur and his men trained in trench

*From the left: Secretary of War Newton Baker,
Major General Tasker Bliss, General William
Mann, Commander of the 42nd Division, and
Colonel MacArthur line up to inspect the newly
formed Rainbow Division at Camp Mills, in 1917.*

warfare. Enemy and Allied troops were dug into
deep, muddy ditches, surrounded by barbed wire.
They suffered from the bitter cold, filth, and constant bombardment. Periodically, one side
charged the other, attempting to cross the "no-
man's-land" between them, to gain a few yards of
territory. Casualties were very high.

On February 20, 1918, MacArthur blackened his face with mud and went out on his first night raid with the French. They hoped to capture Germans to interrogate them about their plans. The men clipped the barbed wire and crawled through mud to reach the enemy trenches, dodging exploding grenades, machine-gun bullets, and artillery fire. Then they engaged

"It's all in the game." in fierce hand-to-hand combat. Returning safely with prisoners, MacArthur was asked why he had risked his life. "It's all in the game," he replied. He received the U.S. silver star for gallantry in action.

The Germans retaliated with a series of raids that cost the Rainbow Division nearly 100 men. On March 9, MacArthur and his men avenged their comrades. They went over the top of the trench and attacked the enemy. For single-handedly wiping out a machine-gun nest, MacArthur won the Distinguished Service Cross (DSC) for extraordinary heroism. This was the first time he had led a charge against the enemy.

AN UNCONVENTIONAL LEADER

MacArthur made himself into a dramatic, easily recognizable figure to his men—and to the enemy.

MacArthur's taste for non-regulation clothing sometimes caused him to be mistaken for a German officer. According to some sources, he was captured by his own men during the Argonne offensive.

Instead of the regulation battle helmet, he chose an officer's cap and pulled out the supporting wire frame. He often wore a four-foot scarf Pinky had knitted, along with an open-necked shirt, a sweater with his West Point letter, and riding pants. Defying orders, he refused to carry or wear a gas mask, yet he disciplined his men for failing to do so. He was gassed on March 11, 1919, and had to be blindfolded for two weeks to save his eyesight. (As a result of its use in World War I, poison gas was banned as a military weapon.) He took few precautions, boasting "All of Germany cannot fabricate the shell that will kill me."

MacArthur's courage was infectious. His men followed wherever he led. They were devoted to him because he shared their hardships and battlefield experiences. As a staff officer, MacArthur could have stayed safely behind the lines, relying on reports from others. Instead he visited the troops to check things out himself. His men knew he would look out for them. For example, he managed to get hot food delivered to them at the front.

A GENERAL AT THE FRONT

On the home front, Pinky had been following her son's career. She traced his movements using his letters and newspaper accounts of his heroism. She began a campaign of her own. She wrote to General Pershing and Secretary Baker to get him

Advancing troops faced enemy fire and clouds of poison gas that burned, and sometimes permanently damaged, their throats. The soldier at the left, without a mask, clutches his throat in pain.

promoted. However, "spit and polish" Pershing did not respect MacArthur's leadership style. During a troop inspection, he had scolded MacArthur for the Rainbow Division's slack discipline and sloppy uniforms. In June, Army Chief of Staff Peyton March, one of his father's former aides, added MacArthur's name to Pershing's promotion list. MacArthur became a brigadier general, the youngest general in the army.

The Rainbow Division saw action in major campaigns of World War I. In March 1918, MacArthur's men fought fiercely in Lorraine, France, for eighty-two days, suffering heavy casualties. During the fighting at Château-Thierry, the new general taught his men Native American tactics he remembered learning in childhood. They crawled forward in pairs, on their bellies, throwing grenades into German machine-gun nests. For his leadership under fire, MacArthur was made commander of the 84th Brigade of the Rainbow Division. The staff officers presented him with a gold cigarette case inscribed to "the bravest of the brave."

In August, the Rainbow Division was ordered to St.-Benoit-en-Woëvre near Verdun. The Germans had held it for four years. Despite a fever, MacArthur led a raid, attacking the Germans' unprotected flanks instead of the center where their strength was concentrated. Then he encouraged the entire division to pursue the enemy, hastening their retreat from the fortified city of Metz.

WAR'S END

In early October, after others had failed, MacArthur's troops repeated the strategy that

The European Campaign during World War I
(stars indicate where MacArthur fought)

The fierce fighting took millions of lives. Here MacArthur (bareheaded, in the center) stands during the playing of "Taps" at a soldier's funeral.

had worked near Metz and took a crucial hill in the heavily defended Côte-de-Châtillon, part of the German defenses known as the Hindenburg Line. The Côte-de-Châtillon was the key to capturing the city of Sedan, a major railroad center. The fierce fighting cost the Rainbow Division 4,000 casualties.

Despite their previous clashes, Pershing now recommended MacArthur for promotion to major general and placed him in temporary command of the Rainbow Division. When the Armistice of November 11, 1918 ended the war, it also ended all promotions. Another division leader of suitable rank was found.

MacArthur was rejected for the Medal of Honor again. Despite his heroism, he had failed to match his father's achievements. When he heard the news, he was bedridden with the flu. However, in March 1919, Pershing awarded him the Dis-

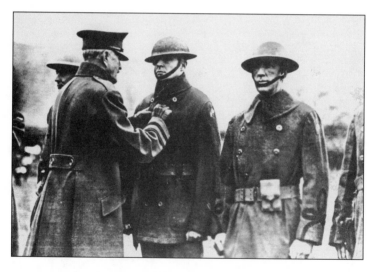

General John J. Pershing (left) awards Brigadier General MacArthur the Distinguished Service Medal in March 1919.

tinguished Service Medal (DSM). It was the highest decoration given to staff officers. Few held the double honor of a DSM and a DSC.

In April, the Rainbow Division was ordered home. World War I had taught MacArthur lessons about leadership and strategy that he had not learned at the Military Academy. West Point would soon benefit from his experiences.

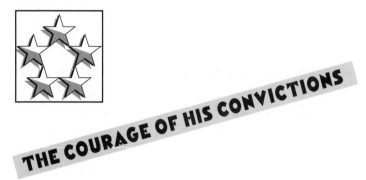

CHAPTER FOUR

THE COURAGE OF HIS CONVICTIONS

"I'm not an educator. I'm a field soldier," MacArthur protested, after being named superintendent of West Point. The secretary of war wanted him to modernize officer training at the military academy. World War I had taught MacArthur that future wars would be highly mechanized, with tanks, machine guns, and planes.

CHANGES AT WEST POINT

With Pinky running his household, the new superintendent got down to work at the academy. He introduced courses in auto mechanics, history, economics, and government. He had the cadets study World War I instead of the Civil War. They were ordered to read a newspaper every day to learn about current events. MacArthur also encouraged them to write poetry to express themselves, and to take dancing lessons, with faculty wives and daughters as their partners, to improve their social skills.

Under MacArthur's leadership, discipline was changed. Remembering the drawbacks of his own life as a cadet, he gave upperclassmen weekend passes away from the academy. Cadets received a $5 allowance each month to spend as they wished. While he did not care about traditional dress codes and military drills, he was concerned about hazing practices. He asked a group of upperclassmen to draw up a new code of conduct. They banned fistfights and deep knee bends over broken glass. West Point had always had an honor code forbidding cadets to steal, lie, or cheat, but it had been enforced by officers. Under MacArthur's reforms, cadets policed themselves.

One of the superintendent's most lasting contributions to West Point was the introduction of intramural athletics, or competitions between classes. His words were carved over the entrance to the gym: "On the fields of friendly strife are sown the seeds that upon other fields and other days will bear the fruits of victory." Cadets were required to participate in at least one of seventeen new sports activities. Ever a passionate football fan, MacArthur even suggested new plays to the coach. His advice was ignored.

President Warren Harding, Secretary of the Army John Weeks, and Brigadier General Douglas MacArthur review the West Point cadets in 1921.

LOVE AT FIRST SIGHT

One September afternoon in 1921, the wealthy socialite Louise Brooks drove up to West Point with a group of army officer friends and was introduced to MacArthur. She was a divorcee with two children. The superintendent and the heiress were strongly attracted to one another. Within a few weeks he proposed, and she accepted. They were married on February 14, 1922, in Palm Beach,

After a happy beginning, the marriage of MacArthur and Louise Brooks foundered. Among other differences, he was always on time, and she was always late.

Florida. Pinky was recovering from a heart attack in a New York City hospital and did not attend.

EXILE IN THE PHILIPPINES

The reforms at West Point angered many graduates, members of Congress, and the academy's board of senior faculty. MacArthur made no effort to win them over. He followed his father's example and never socialized with politicians or with his officers. One of his opponents was General Pershing, a West Point graduate. When Pershing became chief of staff, he ordered MacArthur to the Philippines to take charge of American troops in Manila at the end of the school year in 1922. It was an insulting assignment for a general.

The assignment strained MacArthur's marriage. He enjoyed seeing old friends, including two rising Filipino politicians: Manuel Quezon and Sergio Osmena—but Louise looked down on Filipinos. He hated parties so she went alone. She ignored the other military wives and spent time with wealthy Americans in Manila. In their company, she frequently poked fun at her husband. "Sir Galahad conducted his courtship as if he were conducting a review of a division of his troops," she told them. He spent more time with her children than she did.

In February 1923, Pinky became seriously ill so the MacArthurs rushed back to the United States. By the time they arrived, she had recovered. Both women tried but failed to get MacArthur promoted and transferred home. In June, the MacArthurs went back to Manila and did not return when MacArthur's brother Arthur died of a burst appendix six months later.

Major General Douglas MacArthur walks with leaders of the Philippine legislature—Manuel Quezon, Sergio Osmena, and Manuel Roxas—after assuming command of the Philippine Department in 1925.

In 1924, the general was given duties more suitable to his rank. He was to command the U.S.-trained Filipino Scouts, the island's own soldiers. They welcomed MacArthur's leadership because he treated Filipinos fairly. Along with the U.S. infantry, the Scouts were part of the Philippine Division of the United States Army, receiving the same pay and status as the Americans.

THE COURT-MARTIAL OF BILLY MITCHELL

In January 1925, when Pershing retired as chief of staff, MacArthur was promoted to major general and finally posted stateside. Still seeking to match his father's military record, he applied for a Medal of Honor for his 1914 mission to Veracruz. He was turned down again. In October, he was ordered to serve on the court-martial board at the trial of Brigadier General Billy Mitchell. MacArthur described the assignment as "one of the most distasteful orders I ever received."

Mitchell was an outspoken critic of the armed services. He defied orders to keep his views to himself and bluntly condemned the army and the navy. The air corps served under army and navy commands, but Mitchell wanted it to become an independent service. He insisted that aerial warfare was as important as land or sea combat. He bombed and sank warships in a test to prove his point.

How MacArthur voted in the court-martial is unknown. Nevertheless, some reporters accused him of abandoning a friend; he had known Mitchell for years. MacArthur wrote, "I did what I could in his behalf, and I helped save him from dismissal." Mitchell was suspended from duty for two and a half years, but chose to resign. He continued his crusade to create an independent air corps until his death in 1936.

"I helped save him from dismissal."

PRESIDENT OF THE U.S. OLYMPIC COMMITTEE

In the aftermath of World War I, American life had returned to "normalcy." People were more interested in making and spending money than in preparing for future wars or becoming involved in other nations' problems. This left little for a professional soldier like MacArthur to do.

In 1927, he was invited to become president of the American Olympic Committee. On temporary leave from the army, he escorted the U.S. team to the Olympic Games in Amsterdam in 1928. "We did not come here to lose gracefully," he told them. "We came here to win." The team earned more medals than any other nation. Louise did not accompany her husband, nor did she join him when he was ordered to return to the Philippines to head the Philippine

"We came here to win."

MacArthur (center), with one representative for each sport the American Olympic team entered, on board ship bound for the 1928 games

Department, commanding Filipino and American troops. Instead she traveled to Reno, Nevada, and divorced him on June 18, 1929.

DISBANDING THE BONUS ARMY

On August 5, 1930, President Herbert C. Hoover appointed MacArthur chief of staff. The hesitant general felt that the job would be "a dreadful ordeal." His proud mother cabled him to accept it and prepared to move into the chief's spacious home at Fort Myers, Virginia.

When MacArthur returned stateside he found businesses closing and factories idle. The stock market collapse of 1929 had left millions of Americans jobless, homeless, and hungry in the Great Depression.

During the spring of 1932, about 15,000 unemployed World War I veterans (many with their families) marched to Washington, D.C. Known as the Bonus Army, they came to the capital to demand the pensions that Congress had promised them for wartime service. These pensions had been set up in 1924 but were not payable until 1945. The economy-minded Congress rejected the demands as too costly. Half the disappointed veterans went home. The rest lacked train fare and camped out in vacant government buildings or built shacks in nearby Anacostia Flats.

President Hoover had Congress pass a law allowing the veterans to borrow against their bonuses to get home. Still, the men refused to leave. On July 27, the anxious president ordered the police to clear them from government buildings. The next day violence erupted. Several policemen were injured, and two veterans were killed. The police asked for help.

Secretary of War Patrick Hurley ordered MacArthur to remove the veterans. Against the advice of his aide, future president Dwight D. Eisenhower, MacArthur took charge of the operation himself. Dressed in military uniform, he led four troops of cavalry and four infantry companies equipped with tanks, machine guns, and tear gas. The army drove the veterans from the Capitol building with tear gas and then headed toward Anacostia Flats. MacArthur's men gave the veterans' families two hours to pack and leave. Then the troops crossed the Anacostia Bridge and closed off the camp with little bloodshed. The hundred or so remaining veterans set fire to their shacks. The army left, and the police took over.

At a press conference that night, MacArthur announced that he had saved the country from "revolution." He had defeated radicals who wanted to overthrow the

Saving the country from "revolution."

The aggressive tactics used against the bonus marchers drew a good deal of criticism. Here mounted soldiers drive back Bonus Army marchers.

government. He saw himself as a hero protecting his country. Public opinion, however, favored the veterans.

Many biographers and historians have painted MacArthur as a villain who used excessive force against innocent victims of the Depression, and who crossed the Anacostia Bridge in defiance of the president's orders. This version first appeared in the memoirs of MacArthur's right-wing aide, General Philip Mosely, and has been repeated often.

Hoover and Hurley did instruct MacArthur not to cross the bridge until women and children in the camp were removed, lest they be exposed to tear gas. Only recently has it been learned that Mosely never delivered that order to MacArthur. A worried Hoover repeated the order in a second message, but by the time it arrived, MacArthur's troops had already crossed the bridge.

WORKING WITH FDR

For the next three years, Chief of Staff MacArthur served under his distant relative President Franklin D. Roosevelt. Despite MacArthur's pleas to the Congress, the cost-cutting lawmakers decreased military pay, reduced the size of the army, and refused to fund new tanks or artillery. They did equip the infantry with new semiautomatic rifles.

The general helped the president with a new project—the Civilian Conservation Corps, aimed at putting unemployed youth to work planting trees and digging irrigation ditches. The army set up camps to feed, clothe, and supervise the young men. The success of the camps benefited both the president and his chief of staff, who was awarded a second DSM upon leaving the post in 1935.

A NEW LOVE

MacArthur accepted Manuel Quezon's offer to serve as military advisor to the Philippines and was made a field marshall in the Philippine army. As was common at the time, MacArthur received his army pay and an additional salary from Quezon's government. The Philippines were about to become a commonwealth, as a step toward independence, with Quezon as president. The United States government, however, was still responsible for the islands' defense.

Pinky, MacArthur, and his brother's widow Mary set out for the Philippines. On board ship, the general met Jean Faircloth, a wealthy southern woman from Murfreesboro, Tennessee, who liked to travel. MacArthur wanted to get to know her, but Pinky became ill during the voyage. He devoted most of his time to Pinky, seeing Jean only at breakfast.

> **"Our devoted comradeship of so many years came to an end."**

A month after the MacArthurs settled in Manila, Pinky died of a stroke. MacArthur wrote, "Our devoted comradeship of so many years came to an end." He grieved for months, keeping her Bible near his bed and reading from it every night.

Jean came to Manila to comfort the lonely general. In 1937, when MacArthur accompanied Quezon on a trip to the United States, she traveled to New York. There she and MacArthur were married on April 30. He told reporters, "This is for keeps."

Back in Manila, the fifty-seven-year-old general and his thirty-eight-year-old bride settled into an air-conditioned penthouse at the Manila

MacArthur and his wife, Jean Faircloth

Hotel. In a delicate southern accent, she referred to her husband as the "Gin'ral" or "Sir Boss," from a domineering character in a Mark Twain story. He called her "Ma'am," as if he were addressing a queen.

On February 21, 1938, Jean gave birth to a son, whom they named Arthur. As a young child, Arthur joined his father every morning at 7:30. The two saluted one another and marched around the bedroom shouting "Boom! Boom!" Then the general shaved while singing army songs to his son. He claimed that Arthur was "the only one who appreciates my singing." Every day, when playtime was over, MacArthur gave him gifts, such as crayons or colored pencils. Arthur spent the rest of the day with his Chinese nursemaid and his mother.

"The only one who appreciates my singing."

MacArthur went to the office at midmorning, after breakfasting with Jean. He returned for lunch and a nap, and then went back to work. After dinner, the MacArthurs frequently went to the movies. He preferred Westerns. Occasionally he took his military aides to boxing matches.

The general treated his staff as if they were family. Although usually distant and shy with other officers, he often perched on his aide's desks and asked after their families. In return, he demanded their undivided loyalty. When his aide, Eisenhower, transferred back to the United States in 1939 at the end of his tour of duty, MacArthur could not understand why. Eisenhower, tired of being a staffer behind a desk, hoped to become a field commander, and was looking for a way to earn promotions. World War II was beginning, bringing Germany, Italy, and Japan into conflict with France and Britain—and later the Soviet Union and the United States.

DEFENSE OF THE PHILIPPINES

By the late 1930s, Japanese armies threatened the peace of Asia and the Pacific. The Philippines stood in the sea lanes between Japan and the oil and rubber it needed in Southeast Asia. With 7,000 miles of unprotected coastline, the islands were difficult to defend. According to secret U.S. war plans, the navy was to depart at the first sign of an invasion. The understaffed army was to retreat to Bataan and Corregidor, overlooking Manila Bay, until relief came.

Although publicly committed to defending the Philippines, President Roosevelt and his advisers were privately prepared to sacrifice the islands as indefensible. MacArthur disagreed. He repeatedly demanded that President Roosevelt give him more men and weapons. Instead, Roosevelt offered him any command he desired if he would leave the Philippines. MacArthur decided to retire from the army's active list and advise Quezon. He offered to be reactivated, however, if war threatened.

MacArthur urged Quezon to build up a citizen army of reservists, trained to fight for their country when needed. Unfortunately, the program was not started until late 1941. Even then, shortages left the men without weapons or such basic equipment as shoes and steel helmets. Many recruits could not read and were physically unfit due to poor diets. Still MacArthur planned to have the reservists, the Filipino Scouts, and U.S. troops attack the invaders right on the beaches as they landed.

By 1941, Japanese armies held most Chinese ports and were moving into Southeast Asia. On July 27, the U.S. government reactivated MacArthur as a lieutenant general in command of the United States Armed Forces in the Far East. He did not expect to have to go to war until April 1942, but he was soon proven wrong.

CHAPTER FIVE

A PROMISE KEPT

"Pearl Harbor! It should be our strongest point!" MacArthur exclaimed. He had just learned about the surprise Japanese bombing attack on the American naval base in Hawaii. On December 7, 1941, most of the heavy ships of the U.S. Pacific fleet had been sunk or badly damaged. The next day, the United States declared war on Japan. As allies of Japan, Germany and Italy immediately joined the enemy camp.

Japanese planes struck the Philippines on December 8. MacArthur and his officers were the victims of bad luck, bad timing, and poor judgment. Despite MacArthur's defense plans, the Japanese wiped out the islands' only radar station and wrecked sixteen bombers refueling on the ground. Inexperienced Filipino troops disappeared as soon as enemy soldiers landed on the beaches. Once the main force of Japanese troops

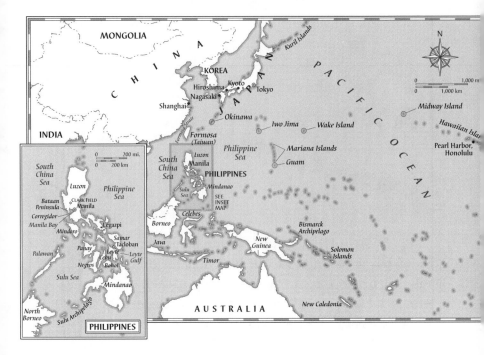

The Pacific Theater in World War II

arrived, MacArthur fell back on the army plan he had bitterly criticized in the past. He would hold Bataan and Corregidor until help came.

RETREAT TO BATAAN AND CORREGIDOR

On Christmas Eve, the MacArthurs arrived at the tiny rocky island of Corregidor in Manila Bay. In the 1930s, as a defensive measure, MacArthur had ordered construction of the 1,500-foot Malinta Tunnel, built into a hill on the island. Now it served as his headquarters.

In their haste to get to Corregidor, MacArthur left behind his beloved books, while Jean abandoned her family silver. However, Arthur managed to take his stuffed rabbit. Dressed in his own military uniform, he ran through the tunnel

Young Arthur MacArthur, dressed in his soldier's uniform, poses at the entrance to the Malinta Tunnel on Corregidor.

shouting, "Air raid! Air raid!" He soon became the mascot of Corregidor's soldiers and army nurses.

MacArthur arranged an orderly evacuation of his troops from Luzon Island to the Bataan Peninsula, two miles north of Corregidor. He was familiar with Bataan's rugged hills and jungle, having surveyed the area as a young officer. Following his plans, the troops withdrew, took up defensive positions, held them long enough to delay the Japanese, then fell back to the next position. Their retreat was so successful that it was studied by officers after the war.

Unfortunately, the army plan never anticipated the arrival of so many troops and refugees on Bataan. There were serious shortages of food and munitions. The defenders of Bataan had only a twenty-day supply of rice and lived on half-rations with no fresh meat or fruit. As a result, the hungry men soon came down with tropical diseases that further weakened them.

On January 9, 1942, MacArthur went to Bataan and visited the troops for the first and only time. They nicknamed him "Dugout Doug" because they felt he kept to the safety of headquarters and avoided the perils of the front lines. Perhaps he made only one visit because he knew there was little he could do for the men. He relayed a message from U.S. Chief of Staff George

C. Marshall on January 15, "Help is on the way." Help did not arrive.

Despite U.S. government promises of men and munitions, MacArthur received little support. Shipments from the United States to the Philippines had to travel enormous distances. The U.S. Pacific Fleet had been badly damaged, and long-range planes did not yet exist. Also, while rearming, the U.S. government gave the war in Europe priority over the war in the Pacific. Submarines and blockade runners brought in some supplies from Australia, but the Japanese navy made such trips dangerous.

On February 20, ailing President Manuel Quezon and his family were evacuated from Corregidor and taken to safety by submarine. Sent with them for safekeeping was MacArthur's footlocker, packed with his medals, personal documents, mementos, and a $500,000 bonus from Quezon. The money was for his services as field marshal, the arrangement made back in 1935.

A NARROW ESCAPE

On February 23, President Roosevelt ordered MacArthur to Australia. The president would not risk letting him be captured or killed by the Japanese. To the American public, the general was a hero. Reporters featured him in stories on the brave defenders of the Philippines.

MacArthur thought about resigning from the army and staying with his men. If he left, however, he might be able to lead fresh troops back to Bataan to relieve them. He decided to leave. Concerned about the men's morale, he requested permission to pick his departure date. The troops were still defending Bataan, aided by Filipino guerrillas, but they could not hold out much longer.

On March 11, MacArthur told the officers who were staying behind, "I want you to make it known . . . that I'm leaving over my repeated protests." After their goodbyes, the MacArthurs and key aides set out on the dangerous trip by armed patrol boat, sneaking past Japanese ships to a landing strip on the island of Mindanao. Then a bomber flew them 3,000 miles to Australia. Describing his narrow escape from the Philippines to reporters, MacArthur uttered a phrase that would become famous: "I shall return." At first, MacArthur thought he would bring relief to the Philippines by summer, but two years passed before he could keep his word.

"I'm leaving over my repeated protests."

On April 9, with food and ammunition dwindling, the men on Bataan surrendered to the

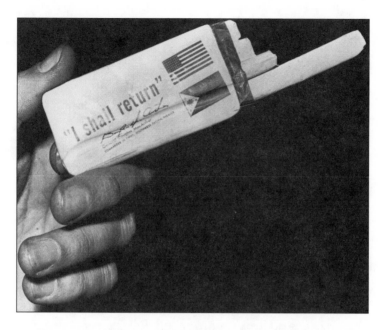

Cigarette packs carrying MacArthur's pledge and signature were dropped from Allied planes to inspire Filipino guerrillas in the days before the invasion of Luzon.

advancing enemy. Despite heavy bombardment, Corregidor held out for another month. Then the survivors were forced on the infamous Death March back up the Bataan Peninsula to prison camps. Illness, meager rations, and the enemy's brutality took thousands of lives.

The bravery of the embattled soldiers became a call to arms. It also brought MacArthur the

Medal of Honor. In defeat, he won the decoration he had long wanted. From Australia, MacArthur commented, "I shall always seem to see a vision of grim, gaunt, ghastly men, still unafraid."

LEAPFROGGING OVER THE PACIFIC

From his base in Australia, MacArthur was commander-in-chief of the Southwest Pacific Area. The region was about as large as the United States, with 12,000 miles of coastline. It included Australia, the Bismark Archipelago, Borneo, the Dutch East Indies, New Guinea, the Philippines, and the Solomon Islands. Most of the vast Pacific remained under navy command. Longtime rivals, the army and navy competed for scarce supplies and argued for their own strategies. They did cooperate, however, in some campaigns against the Japanese.

Half of New Guinea, the world's second largest island, was under Japanese control. This posed a threat to Australia. The Japanese wanted to capture Port Moresby, the only large town on the island, located on its eastern tip. The American naval victory in the Battle of the Coral Sea kept the Japanese from bringing troops to the town by water. For the next nine months, MacArthur's troops fought to keep Japanese forces from taking the town by land. Both sides

Filipino guerrillas, fighting with U.S. troops on Leyte, practice using their traditional weapons, bolos.

were battling dense jungles, a hot, humid climate, and difficult mountain trails.

The general ordered his field commanders to strike the enemy from the rear and the sides rather than head on. He advised his soldiers, "When the Japanese soldier has a coordinated plan of attack, he works smoothly. When he is attacked—when he doesn't know what is coming—it isn't the same." Nevertheless, both sides took heavy losses as the fighting continued.

General George Kenney, MacArthur's air commander, convinced him to use airplanes to bombard the enemy and to transport troops. MacArthur went along on the first parachute drop. "I'm not worried about getting shot," he insisted, but added, "I'd hate to get sick and disgrace myself in front of the kids." He added a leather flight jacket to his irregular uniform.

"I'd hate to get sick and disgrace myself in front of the kids."

MacArthur's wife and son stayed with him in Australia until he moved his headquarters nearer the front lines. Haunted by memories of Bataan and the bloody battle for New Guinea, he turned to his family for comfort. Because the general still did not like to socialize, Jean substituted for him. For example, she entertained Eleanor Roosevelt when the First Lady visited Australia.

The hard-working general kept his staff busy. To relax, MacArthur watched Westerns, often inviting his aides to join him. A clean-desk man, he saved few papers. He preferred talking to writing, but he did write frequently to Earl "Red" Blaik, coach of the West Point football team. MacArthur was delighted to receive movies of the games. He critiqued them in his letters back to the coach.

In March 1943, Kenney's bombers destroyed Japanese troop transports headed for New Guinea in the Battle of the Bismark Sea. Thus the enemy could no longer reinforce its bases by sea. Since U.S. intelligence had broken the Japanese communications code, the army and navy could bypass heavily fortified, enemy-held islands. Instead they attacked and captured weaker outposts and built airfields on them in preparation for their next advance.

This strategy was known as leapfrogging. It isolated Japanese strongholds, breaking their lines of supply and communication. MacArthur's men needed nine months to clear enemy troops from the northeast coast of New Guinea and cut off the main Japanese base at Rabaul. By leapfrogging, it took them only three months to move 1,400 miles to the Admiralty Islands and the Moluccas, just 300 miles from the Philippines.

MacArthur was determined to retake the Philippines. The navy preferred to strike Formosa, off the coast of China. MacArthur asked whether President Roosevelt was willing "to accept responsibility for breaking a promise to eighteen million Christian Filipinos that the Americans would return?" MacArthur, not Roosevelt, had made that promise. In July 1944, the president met with representatives of the navy and General MacArthur in Hawaii to discuss the problem. In early October, Roosevelt told the general to go ahead. The president's military advisers had informed him that there weren't enough American troops available in the Pacific to take Formosa. After the war, historians questioned whether the liberation of the Philippines had been necessary.

RETURN TO THE PHILIPPINES

At 10 A.M. October 20, 1944, American troops landed at Tacloban, the regional capital of Leyte, with few casualties. From the deck of the *Nashville*, MacArthur saw that the docks he had built in 1903 were still standing. That afternoon, accompanied by reporters and the new president of the Philippines, Sergio Osmena, he waded ashore. Against a background of artillery fire, the general announced over the radio, "People of the Philippines: I have returned. ... Rally to me."

"Rally to me."

MacArthur's troops faced heavy Japanese resistance inland, and, despite help from guerillas, the campaign dragged on until the spring of 1945. On December 18, 1944, MacArthur was promoted to the rank of General of the Army, an honor he shared with Marshall and Eisenhower.

A famous photograph commemorated the return of MacArthur (third from left) to the Philippines, as he waded ashore at Leyte, during the first landings of American troops in October 1944.

THE FIGHT FOR MANILA

On January 8, 1945, MacArthur's troops hit the northern beaches on Luzon Island. The troops fought their way south to Manila. Meanwhile the Japanese army retreated into the hills north of the capital and dug in. Japanese naval officers, however, were determined to hold Manila. From doorways, rooftops, and alleys, their forces fought the American invaders for over a month. MacArthur had refused to let Manila be bombed because too many civilians would be killed. Nevertheless, both sides resorted to heavy artillery fire and reduced the once beautiful city to rubble. About 100,000 civilians died.

MacArthur toured the ruins of his penthouse home in the Manila Hotel. All his possessions had been destroyed. However, he was given a Japanese officer's trunk labeled "Medical Supplies." Inside were his tea set, bowls, and Jean's treasured silver candlesticks. He soon settled into a new home named Casa Blanca (white house)—an odd coincidence because he had recently lost a chance to live in the White House in Washington, D.C. He had been approached to become the Republican nominee for president in 1944, but little came of it.

MacArthur's wife and son arrived on March 6 from Australia, along with Phyllis Gibbons,

Arthur's tutor. While soldiers and Filipinos worked side-by-side to restore the city, Jean visited military hospitals.

By March 2, both Bataan and Corregidor were once more in American hands. The fighting had been fierce on Corregidor. Over 2,000 Japanese troops had blown themselves up in Malinta Tunnel rather than surrender. Meanwhile MacArthur ordered raids to free prisoners from Japanese prison camps. While the army slowly retook northern Luzon from the Japanese, the rest of the Philippines fell more quickly into American hands. MacArthur received his third DSC.

COLLABORATORS

MacArthur had to decide what to do about Filipinos who had collaborated, or worked with, the enemy. Nearly all the governing class, including two of Osmena's sons, had had business dealings with the Japanese. President Roosevelt had wanted collaborators to be treated harshly. His successor, President Harry S. Truman, let MacArthur handle the problem.

The general stated, "It is hardly fair for us . . . [to] judge or criticize people for employing almost any means to save their own lives and the lives of their families." For example, Manuel Roxas, a popular Filipino politician, had served the Japanese as minister of food. When MacArthur interviewed Filipino guerrillas, he learned that Roxas actually helped them during the occupation, while seeming to assist the enemy. Roxas would become the first president of the independent Philippine Republic. On August 23, 1945, 6,000 collaborators would be placed in the charge of the Philippine government.

"Men like me are obsolete. There will be no more wars."

In June the general ordered troops to take Borneo from the Japanese. In mid July, he was briefed about the atomic bomb, a powerful new weapon of mass destruction. After it had been used by the United States to wipe out the cities of Hiroshima and Nagasaki, he told a reporter, "Men like me are obsolete. There will be no more wars."

The American government did not think he was obsolete. On August 15, President Truman named him Supreme Commander for Allied Powers, with orders to accept the surrender of Japan and to oversee the occupation of the defeated nation.

CHAPTER SIX

THE AMERICAN WAY

"Never in history had a nation and its people been more completely crushed," MacArthur commented. All around him he saw rubble and ruin. He set up headquarters in Tokyo, Japan's capital, in the Dai Ichi (the big one) Building. It was one of the few structures to survive the American bombings.

Each morning, he rode slowly to work in an unescorted car bearing the U.S. flag. Despite his staff's fears, he did not think the Japanese would harm him. From his 1905 visit to Japan and his reading about the Far East, he considered himself an expert on Asia. He was certain he could handle the Japanese in a way that they would accept.

The Japanese military had run the country for decades. Even before that the public had had no part in government or politics. Powerful noble families had controlled Japanese life. Now the Japanese were a devastated people ready for

Tokyo's rubble demonstrates the force of the Allied bombings.

change. Most were shocked by their defeat. Their leaders had lied to them, never admitting that they were losing the war. The people also learned that their army had abused conquered peoples and prisoners.

Few Japanese had ever seen the current emperor, Hirohito, or heard his voice, until the surrender.

He lived in the palace with his family and was seen only by his ministers and servants. Japanese emperors had always been regarded as gods. On January 1, 1946, Emperor Hirohito declared, as required by the Allies, that he was not divine.

KEEPING HIS DISTANCE

On September 8, MacArthur moved into the U.S. Embassy and sent for his wife and son. Once settled, the MacArthurs lived much as they had in the Philippines before the war. The general avoided official parties and only met visiting American officials and journalists over lunch. In 1946, however, the MacArthurs did give a formal dinner for Dwight Eisenhower, the new chief of staff.

Like the Japanese emperor, MacArthur kept himself apart from the people. He did not socialize with the Japanese. As the new, temporary ruler of Japan, he behaved in a way the Japanese could understand. He did not tour the countryside. To gain information, he sent his wife to different parts of the nation and asked her to report on what she saw. In addition, a military cameraman filmed Japanese life. The general watched these films at night, along with his favorite Westerns and West Point football films.

MacArthur was ordered to turn Japan into a democratic nation, giving political power to the

The Japanese emperor—considered a god—lived apart from the people inside the palace grounds. This 1928 photograph shows Emperor Hirohito in his coronation robe.

people. Never before had a conqueror attempted such extensive and permanent changes in a defeated nation. The directives MacArthur received from Washington, however, were not specific. "My major advisers now have boiled down almost to two men," he told a visiting journalist, "George Washington and Abraham Lincoln. One founded the United States, the other saved it. If you go back into their lives, you can find almost all the answers." He ignored Allied advisory groups set up to give recommendations and to check on his progress. The U.S. government let him do this as long as his actions did not conflict with its aims.

"My major advisers now [are] George Washington and Abraham Lincoln."

On September 28, 1945, Hirohito visited MacArthur. During their conversation, the emperor offered to support the general's reforms. MacArthur ordered every Japanese newspaper to publish a photograph of their unique meeting, which helped make the occupation acceptable to the people. Japanese government officials had already agreed to cooperate with the general. He was pleased because he wanted the Japanese to help shape their own future.

This photograph of the historic meeting between MacArthur and Hirohito appeared in Japanese newspapers.

BREAKING WITH THE PAST

One of MacArthur's first concerns was to disarm Japan's 7 million soldiers. He made the unusual decision to allow Japanese officers to collect their troops' weapons instead of using the U.S. Army to do it. This act lessened the former enemy's humiliation and anger. His plan was so successful that by December he needed only 200,000 occupation troops. The rest were sent home, to the delight of their families.

President Truman was outraged by MacArthur's announcement that he did not need a large occupation force. The president was trying to get a peacetime draft passed by using the occupation as an excuse. Twice Truman suggested, but did not order, that MacArthur come home. He wanted him to be briefed on current issues. The general declined. He was reluctant to leave Japan, and he disliked flying. (MacArthur left Japan only on July 4, 1946, to visit the Philippines on their independence day, and on August 15, 1948, to attend the swearing in of Syngman Rhee as president of South Korea.) Instead, Truman sent representatives to MacArthur.

Truman and MacArthur shared the determination to prosecute Japanese war criminals. In late 1945, tribunals were set up to try Japanese officers for "crimes against humanity." MacArthur personally arranged for General Tomoyuki Yamashita to be brought to trial. This military leader was accused of failing to prevent the massacre of Filipinos and the destruction of Manila. Yet, Yamashita had retreated from the city long before the crimes were committed. MacArthur could have reduced his sentence but did not. "I have reviewed the proceedings in vain, searching for some mitigating circumstances on his behalf. I can find none." Yamashita was hanged in February 1946. MacArthur also refused to spare the life of Masaharu Homma, who was judged responsible for the Bataan Death March and was executed.

The International Military Tribunal for the Far East charged twenty-eight Japanese with war crimes. One of MacArthur's aides suggested they be exiled, which was how MacArthur's father had treated Filipino guerillas at the turn of the century. MacArthur replied, "Our allies want blood, and our people want blood. . . . I can't stop it."

"I can't stop it."

MacArthur was also ordered to remove from office members of the government suspected of war crimes or active support of the defeated military regime. In January 1946, 400 Japanese lawmakers were dismissed. Over 700,000 Japanese were screened and 200,000 were barred from public life. At the end of 1946, many Japanese in the media, industry, and local government lost their jobs.

GUARANTEES OF FREEDOM

On October 4, 1945, MacArthur ordered the release of about 500 political prisoners. He also disbanded the Japanese secret police. They had arrested anyone who criticized the Japanese government. They had also imprisoned, without trial, people suspected of disloyalty. The general and his staff introduced to Japan the Western idea of *habeas corpus*, which requires an arresting officer to explain to a judge why a prisoner is being held in custody. MacArthur's father had brought this legal protection to the Philippines.

At the same time, the Japanese were given freedom of speech, the right to assemble, and the right to join the political party of their choice. The Japanese government put these reforms into effect. Yet MacArthur felt the need to limit freedom of the press. Some Americans criticized MacArthur for telling the press which stories to feature and which to omit. "Under the Occupation," he explained, "there are some of our policies that we can't let them criticize, because that would make it too difficult for us to carry them out."

MAKING JAPAN A DEMOCRACY

In October 1945, the government started to revise the constitution of 1889, but it did not go far enough to satisfy MacArthur and his staff. The general wrote down what he wanted, and his staff made the changes. They were guided by British and American models. They created a representative democracy with the emperor as a figurehead.

The nobility was removed from the traditional Japanese lawmaking body, the Diet. It became "the highest organ of state power, and was to be made up of elected representatives." MacArthur made sure that the lawmakers truly represented the people by giving all citizens age twenty or older the right to vote. Like the British system of government, the Japanese prime minister and the cabinet (the heads of government departments) proposed new laws and were responsible for putting them into effect. Government workers within the departments were no longer responsible to the emperor. They were now public servants.

An American feature was added to the court system. The highest court could review any law or official act to make sure it did not violate the constitution. Other parts of the constitution guaranteed civil liberties, such as freedom of speech, and required employers and unions to bargain in good faith. An important feature of the constitution was Article Nine, in which the Japanese people permanently gave up the right to go to war.

In March 1946, the constitution went into effect. To make it more acceptable to the Japanese, MacArthur claimed, "The new Japanese constitution is merely an amendment to the older [1889] one." Of course, it was not. The Americans had abolished the Japanese nobility. The constitution shifted political power to the people and safeguarded their new liberties. It took away the emperor's power and made him a symbol of the country, much like the monarch of Britain.

SOCIAL AND ECONOMIC DEMOCRACY

In prewar Japan, women had no political, economic, or legal rights. They attended single-sex schools and did not receive a college education. Under MacArthur's direction, women were given new freedoms, including the right to divorce their husbands, own property, and vote. Educational reforms made high schools coeducational and created women's universities. By the third year of the Occupation, it became customary for a woman to be included in the prime minister's cabinet.

During the winter of 1945–1946, millions of Japanese were starving. The rice harvest had been poor. The general wired Washington, "Give me bread or give me bullets," fearing that the crisis would spark an uprising. American politicians were not eager to feed the former enemy. So MacArthur took food from army storehouses in the Pacific. This crisis proved to him the importance of land reform. Most farmers worked land belonging to absentee owners and gave much of

"Give me bread or give me bullets."

what they grew to these owners. By October 1946, MacArthur had the Japanese Diet pass laws requiring owners to sell their land to the farmers at low prices. The farmers were now free to grow and sell their own crops.

Washington ordered the general to dissolve the huge companies that dominated Japanese industry. The fifteen largest companies had been run by a few families with ties to the Japanese military regime. They controlled the production of chemicals, steel, and machinery. MacArthur broke up the companies and removed more than 1,000 executives and managers from their jobs.

MacArthur opposed giving away Japan's manufacturing equipment and supplies. He believed the country needed them to support itself in the postwar world. Despite his objections, the companies' machinery was taken apart and given to the victorious Allies as payment for the losses they had suffered during the war. The United States, however, took nothing and gave Japan $2 billion in economic assistance.

MacArthur also set out to reform the labor movement. Before the war, there had been only twelve unions, with a total of about 100,000 members. Following the general's orders, the Diet made it easier to form and join unions. MacArthur invited American labor leaders to Japan to help set them up. Between 1945 and 1948, more than 6.6 million Japanese became union members in more than 30,000 labor organizations. They organized numerous strikes for better pay and working conditions.

By 1947, Communists had taken control of some Japanese unions. Following the example of the Soviet Union, Communists wanted the state to do away with private property and to take over all industries in the name of the people. They ignored the fact that the Soviet Union was a brutal dictatorship. Japanese Communists threatened a nationwide strike that would bring the economy to a standstill. When the Diet refused to act, MacArthur stepped in and banned the strike. The workers accepted a pay increase that they had turned down earlier. Before he left Japan, the general removed the Communists from the labor movement. Events in China, as well as in Japan, probably influenced this action.

ASIAN COMMUNISM

In 1945 MacArthur and others predicted that the Chinese Communists of Mao Zedong would defeat the Nationalist troops of Chiang Kai-shek. The two sides had been fighting on and off since 1931. During World War II, Americans had given arms and money to Chiang. After the war, they tried unsuccessfully to get the two sides to negotiate. In August 1949, Chiang was forced to retreat to the island of Formosa. The U.S. government announced that it would not provide him with military aid or defend his regime because it did not want to become involved in the Chinese civil war.

MacArthur had watched the conflict from Japan. In his reports to the U.S. government, he worried that the Communists would eventually threaten U.S. interests in the Pacific region. Chiang's regime was corrupt, but MacArthur urged the government to continue to back it with arms and aid. "If he has horns and a tail, so long as he is anti-Communist, we should help him."

"so long as he is anti-Communist, we should help him."

The general's views were supported by conservative Republicans. They, too, wanted the government to protect Formosa. They went further than the general and blamed the Democratic Truman administration for the fall of China to communism. They charged that the government had given its attention to defending Western Europe from Soviet communism and had neglected Asia. During the fierce debates over American policy toward China, MacArthur remained silent. A year later, after the Communists had turned Korea into a battlefield, he spoke out.

CHAPTER SEVEN

A RISKY BUSINESS

"I had an uncanny feeling of nightmare," MacArthur wrote. The seventy-year-old general, asleep in his quarters in Tokyo, had been awakened by an urgent phone call early in the morning of June 25, 1950. Thousands of North Korean troops were invading South Korea.

At the end of World War II, the Korean peninsula had been unintentionally divided. Japanese troops north of the 38th parallel in Korea surrendered to the Soviet army. Those south of the line turned themselves over to the Americans. In 1948, the Soviet Union refused to allow the United Nations to hold free elections in North Korea to reunite the nation. Elections did take place in the South, creating the Republic of Korea, with Seoul as its capital city. The Soviets quickly set up the Democratic People's Republic of North Korea, with Pyongyang as its capital. Both North and

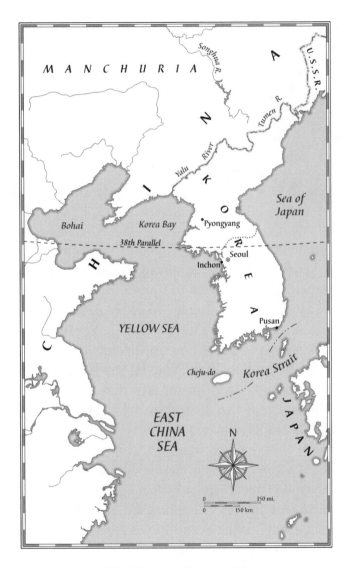

The Korean Peninsula

South Korea claimed to rule all of the country. In 1949, Soviet and American forces withdrew, making a civil war likely.

At first, MacArthur was told to ship arms to the South Korean army (the ROKs). By June 27, he had to fly American personnel out of the country. The North Koreans had captured Seoul, routing the ROK troops. MacArthur cabled Washington, "Complete collapse is imminent." At this point, Truman decided to enter the war. On behalf of the United Nations, the United States agreed to a "police" action in Korea to restore the peace.

> **"Complete collapse is imminent."**

DISAGREEMENTS OVER FORMOSA

On June 28, Truman appointed MacArthur commander-in-chief, Far East. The general was instructed to limit the war to South Korea. He was told to use the Seventh Fleet to patrol the Formosa Strait and keep the Chinese Nationalists and the Chinese Communists apart. In July, he also received the title of UN commander. He eventually took charge of troops from sixteen UN member nations.

MacArthur ordered air strikes against enemy forces in South Korea. On June 29, he flew there to see the situation for himself, the first of seventeen visits he would make to the front. He was not impressed with the fighting abilities of the ROK troops. At MacArthur's urgent request, Truman allowed him to use American ground troops to defend Pusan at the tip of the Korean peninsula. The general claimed, "We win here, or we lose everywhere. But if we win here, we improve our chances of winning everywhere."

From Formosa, Chiang Kai-shek volunteered 33,000 men to support South Korea, but the Communist regime in China supported North Korea and Truman again did not want to involve the U.S. in the Chinese civil war. MacArthur agreed with Truman's decision and flew to Formosa to explain it to Chiang. The visit enraged Truman. It appeared as if MacArthur were backing Chiang. Conservative Republicans, fans of MacArthur, kept pressuring Truman to protect Formosa. So the general was ordered to send a military mission to determine Chiang's needs.

Then MacArthur sent a controversial message to an American veterans group and distributed copies to United States publications hostile to Truman. He stated that Formosa was strategically important to the United States. Reporters made it seem as if there were two U.S. policies toward Formosa, the president's and the general's. An angry Truman ordered MacArthur to withdraw his statement and he did.

A DARING RAID

MacArthur asked for and got reinforcements of American troops in South Korea. He summed up his strategy as "Trade space for time." American forces dug in around Pusan. Despite heavy enemy fire, they held

"Trade space for time."

their ground. The general wanted a rapid victory to keep the Chinese or Soviets from entering the war in support of North Korea. His goal was to cut off the North's supply lines, forcing them to return to the 38th parallel. To do this, he had to attack them from the rear.

MacArthur masterminded the most brilliant maneuver of his career. Americans would land at Inchon, the second largest city in South Korea. This plan was risky because the tides varied by thirty feet. There were no beaches, just sea walls. When the tide went out, ships could become grounded on muddy banks. So the landing had to take place in two stages. First, on the morning of September 15, marines seized Wolmi-do Island, guarding Inchon. MacArthur went ashore while shells were still flying. Second, that afternoon, marines successfully landed at Inchon and quickly took the poorly defended city.

Following the victory at Inchon, Truman flew to Wake Island in the Pacific to meet MacArthur on October 15. The trip was intended to boost Truman's and his party's popularity in the upcoming elections. MacArthur chose to show disrespect for his commander-in-chief. He wanted the president's plane to land first so that Truman would have to welcome him. His plan failed, and he had to greet the president, which was proper.

The conference accomplished little, but Truman did give MacArthur his fourth DSM. Truman asked MacArthur some questions, jumping from topic to topic. The two men spent little time on the possibility of Chinese intervention in Korea. They should have paid more attention to the question.

A DANGEROUS DECISION

Communist China had sent a message through Indian diplomats warning the U.S. to stay out of North Korea. Otherwise, the Chinese would enter the war. Neither Truman nor MacArthur took this threat seriously. With the North Koreans in retreat, MacArthur was instructed to pursue them across the 38th parallel and to use only ROK troops, not U.S. forces, as he approached areas bordering on the Soviet Union or China.

The general divided his troops into two commands. Truman's military advisers thought this was a bad idea, but they were hesitant to question the judgment of such a famous military strategist. The general took this action because he had doubts about one of his commanders. He did not want to give him too much responsibility, nor did he want to dismiss him.

MacArthur violated orders and used Americans in border areas. He claimed that he did not have enough ROK troops and was not reprimanded. Meanwhile, about 100,000 Chinese troops sneaked across the Yalu River into North Korea. On October 25, MacArthur answered with an aerial barrage, knocking out North Korean bridges and communications. Washington had ordered him not to bomb the Chinese side of the bridges, but once more, he defied orders. The U.S. government insisted that he limit future attacks to North Korea. Suddenly the Chinese forces melted away.

Then, on a visit to the front on November 24, MacArthur casually commented that the troops

Home "in time for Christmas."

might be home "in time for Christmas." Reporters turned this remark into an official statement. Before returning to Tokyo, the general flew over the Yalu River. From that altitude, he saw no signs of the Chinese.

However, on November 25, in bitter winter weather, 300,000 Chinese launched a massive drive, pushing the invading Americans and South Koreans southward through the mountains. American casualties were very heavy. Despite superior U.S. air and artillery power, they could not stop the Chinese.

DISMISSING THE GENERAL

At the end of November, MacArthur gave an interview to reporters. He blamed the retreat on the U.S. government, claiming it had restricted his actions against the Chinese. Truman was furious. On December 6, he issued an order requiring military and civil officials to clear press statements with the government.

The general continued to ask the government for more troops to keep U.S. forces from being wiped out or evacuated. In January, the North Koreans captured Seoul, but their supply lines were stretched too far. Despite MacArthur's fears of a military disaster, in February the U.S. Army began a counterattack. It was successful and

Seoul was recaptured in March. Soon the Chinese were driven back across the 38th parallel.

The U.S. government and its UN allies thought it was time to negotiate a settlement and told MacArthur. He wanted to win the war so that his career would not end with a stalemate. Without consulting Washington, the general sent his own offer to the Chinese, deliberately choosing words that would offend them. In effect, he told them to quit or risk being destroyed. Truman was outraged. He wanted to fire the general, but the public applauded MacArthur's bold stand. The general gave interviews to reporters, criticizing the government's position and the restrictions imposed on him.

Early in March, MacArthur had replied to a letter from the Republican leader, Congressman Joseph Martin. Martin had asked for his views on the Korean situation. MacArthur wrote, "There is no substitute for victory," rejecting the possibility of a negotiated settlement. Martin read the letter to Congress on April 5. Truman wrote in a private memo, "This looks like the last straw. Rank insubordination." Rank insubordination is a serious and punishable military offense.

"This looks like the last straw."

On April 10, Truman officially dismissed MacArthur. He feared that MacArthur would hear about his decision through the grapevine and resign. Truman was determined to fire him first. The president called a press conference at 1:00 A.M. to make the announcement. One of MacArthur's aides heard about it on the radio and told the general. He was not surprised. The official papers arrived on April 12. Calmly he told his wife, "Jeannie, we're going home at last." Later he complained about the way he had been fired. "No office boy, no charwoman, no servant of any sort would have been dismissed with such callous disregard for the ordinary decencies." MacArthur seemed to conveniently forget that he had defied the president's orders.

A HERO'S WELCOME

MacArthur was treated as a departing hero and received a nineteen-gun salute. His replacement, Matthew P. Ridgway, gave him a glowing farewell speech. With their heads bowed to show respect, 250,000 Japanese lined the streets along his route to the airport outside Tokyo. Upon arrival in San Francisco late at night, another 500,000 people greeted him and his family. This was the first time his son, Arthur, had set foot on the United

The startling announcement of Truman's firing of MacArthur made headlines around the world. Here the scene is a London news vendor's street corner.

MacArthur, waving, enjoys a shower of ticker tape and the cheers of crowds in a New York City parade.

States mainland. The next day, the MacArthurs took off for Washington, D.C.

The general had been invited to address Congress. Millions of Americans stayed at their television sets to watch and hear his hour and a half speech. MacArthur felt that China, not the Soviet Union, had been the force behind the Korean War and that only American economic and military power would be able to stop China. The general urged the government to support and defend Formosa. He complained about the unreasonable restrictions placed on his command during the war. After fifty-two years in military service, he was not willing to accept anything less than victory.

The speech was interrupted several times with bursts of applause. Near the end, he quoted a line from an old West Point song: "Old soldiers never die; they just fade away." Republicans and Democrats alike gave him a standing ovation. MacArthur visited New York, Milwaukee, and other cities. He was given ticker-tape parades and a hero's welcome. The crowds began to thin, however, after the nation learned more about the general's conduct in Korea.

On May 3, Congress held hearings on the war. The general was the first witness. He claimed that his views had been supported by the president's military advisers. Their testimony contradicted him. The public began to believe that Truman had reason to fire MacArthur. He was described as an "out-of-control general who was pressing a course of action almost certain to ignite World War III."

From then on, the government ignored him.

"Perhaps someone just forgot to remember."

He was not asked to attend the signing of the peace treaty with Japan in San Francisco on September 8, 1951. He had been urging such a

MacArthur, with his wife Jean, waves to the crowd at a New York Giants baseball game in 1951.

pact for several years. "Perhaps someone just forgot to remember," MacArthur commented.

In 1952, he hoped to become the Republican candidate for president. He had failed to win the nomination in 1948. This time, however, conservative Republicans united behind Senator Robert Taft and supported MacArthur as his vice president. They did not have enough votes to succeed. MacArthur's former aide Dwight Eisenhower became the party's candidate and, soon, the nation's president.

MacArthur claimed to have a secret plan to end the war. He would discuss it only with the new president. Meanwhile Eisenhower traveled to Korea, keeping a campaign pledge to see for himself what was going on. Upon his return, he went to see MacArthur. The general recommended that the United States dump nuclear waste on North Korea or threaten China with a nuclear attack to end the war. These proposals were too dangerous and impractical to be taken seriously. A cease-fire brought an end to the Korean conflict on July 27, 1953. MacArthur's political hopes had ended. His advice had been ignored. What was an old soldier to do with the rest of his life?

CHAPTER EIGHT

AN OLD SOLDIER

"I have enjoyed to the full the relaxation of release from the arduous responsibilities of high national command," MacArthur insisted. He and his family moved into the luxurious Waldorf Hotel in New York City. The general served on the board of directors of the Remington Rand Company, now Unisys. The company did most of its business with the military and benefited from MacArthur's fame and his advice on foreign affairs.

He attended the theater and opera with his wife. He also spent hours watching boxing matches on television with former members of his staff and rarely missed a West Point football game. Coach Earl Blaik continued to write to him each week, analyzing the previous week's game. Mac-Arthur offered advice on lineups and plays. He looked forward to this old friend's frequent visits.

HONORS AND REUNIONS

The retired general was not forgotten. In 1954, the Japanese government gave him the Grand Cordon of the Order of the Rising Sun, the highest honor it could give to a foreigner and non-head of state. MacArthur claimed that he could "recall no parallel in history where a great nation recently at war has so distinguished its former enemy commander."

When he turned eighty, his health began to fail. He had liver blockages but refused surgery. Yet, as a young man, he had argued that staying healthy was "the first duty of a soldier." On January 26, 1960, his former staff members met, as they did each year, to celebrate his birthday. They feared this would be the last party. He smiled as the roll call was read and each guest stood at attention. His gifts included mementos from World War II. MacArthur then made a surprising recovery.

In April 1961, he met with President John F. Kennedy. The two men got along so well that Kennedy invited him to the White House three months later. The general advised the president not to commit ground forces to Vietnam. He felt America's problems lay in the inner cities, not in Asia.

More reunions and awards came his way. In July, he flew to the Philippines for the fifteenth anniversary of its independence. He thought that this would be the last time he would see the survivors of Bataan and Corregidor.

In 1962, he accepted the Sylvanus Thayer Award from West Point, for outstanding service to his country. By then, he was ill again. In a moving speech, he reviewed the challenges the cadets would face in the space age. He reminded them that they were still expected to fight and to win. They still had to follow the code they had learned at the military academy "[I]n the evening of my memory, always I come back to West Point. Always there echoes in my ears—Duty—Honor—Country." He left his audience teary eyed.

"Duty—Honor—Country."

A NATION MOURNS

Many books were published about MacArthur's career. Feeling that they weren't always accurate, he set out to write his memoirs. He completed them just before he entered Walter Reed Hospital. He had finally agreed to have surgery. He survived two operations but died of kidney and liver failure during a third procedure on April 5, 1964. At military posts around the world, nineteen-gun salutes were fired and flags were lowered to half staff.

Following MacArthur's instructions, a military funeral was held at the 7th Regiment Armory in New York City. He was dressed in his most faded uniform, without decorations. "Whatever I have done that really matters, I've done wearing it. When the time comes, it will be in these that I journey forth."

About 35,000 New Yorkers lined the streets to pay their respects. West Point cadets, a riderless horse, and an honor guard of generals and admirals marched in the procession accompanying his casket to the waiting train, as MacArthur had wished. Millions watched the ceremony on television. President Lyndon B. Johnson and his wife Ladybird embraced Jean and Arthur at the Washington, D.C. station and escorted them to the Capitol. There the general lay in state. The next day, a government plane flew them to Virginia for a final service. The general had asked to be buried at the MacArthur Memorial, an imposing library erected by the city of Norfolk, Virginia, his mother's hometown. This was a fitting resting place for a brilliant general, and an American patriot.

MacArthur was certainly a hero, but he was also a flawed man. His zeal to exceed his father's military achievements drove him to become a successful leader of men and a gifted military strategist. Unfortunately, he was also vain and over-confident, relying too much on his own judg-

The MacArthur Memorial in Norfolk, Virginia

ment. This trait led him to make costly mistakes in the Philippines and elsewhere. MacArthur used his many talents to help win World War II and went on to transform the defeated Japanese war machine into a modern democracy. However, he could not follow the example he had set for the Japanese—that civilians must control the military. Eager for victory, he repeatedly defied orders from his president during the Korean War. For this inexcusable behavior, he was fired. As an outstanding military officer, his achievements were magnificent, his failures all the more disappointing.

1880	Born on January 26 to Arthur MacArthur Jr. and Mary "Pinky" Pinkney Hardy MacArthur at Fort Dodge, Arkansas.
1903	Graduates first in his class at West Point.
1903–5	Assigned to the Philippines before traveling throughout Asia as his father's aide.
1906	Attends engineering school and becomes an aide to President Theodore Roosevelt.
1907–11	Serves in Milwaukee, Wisconsin; Fort Leavenworth, Kansas; Panama; and Texas.
1912	Joins the Army General Staff after the death of his father.
1914	Goes on an intelligence mission to Veracruz, Mexico.
1916	Becomes a military assistant to the secretary of war.
1917–18	Serves as chief of staff of the Rainbow Division in Europe during World War I and takes part in the American occupation of Germany.
1919	Becomes superintendent of West Point.

1922	Marries Louise Brooks on February 14 and returns to the Philippines as commander of the military district of Manila.
1925	Returns stateside and serves as a member of the military panel at the court-martial of Billy Mitchell.
1929	Divorced from Louise and ordered to the Philippines as commander of the Philippines Department.
1930	Appointed army chief of staff.
1932	Leads troops against Bonus Army encampment at Anacostia Flats in Washington, D.C.
1935	Transferred to the Philippines where his mother dies.
1937	Marries Jean Faircloth on April 20 and resigns from the army's active list.
1938	Son, Arthur MacArthur IV, is born on February 21.
1941	Reactivated and takes command of combined U.S. Armed Forces in the Far East in July.
1942	Ordered by President Franklin Roosevelt to leave U.S. and Filipino troops on besieged Corregidor and depart for Australia in March; receives Medal of Honor; named commander-in-chief of the Southwest Pacific Area.
1944	Returns triumphantly to the Philippines.
1945	Becomes Supreme Allied Commander for the Allied Powers in the Pacific and accepts the surrender of Japan; supervises the occupation and democratization of Japan.

1950	Appointed commander-in-chief, Far East, and UN commander, leading American and UN troops to repel North Korean attack on South Korea.
1951	Dismissed by President Harry S. Truman; gives a farewell address to Congress; defends his views before a congressional committee.
1952	Gives keynote speech at Republican National Convention after failing to win the party's presidential nomination, which he also sought in 1944 and 1948.
1964	Completes the writing of his memoirs, *Reminiscences*; dies on April 5.

Communism A system of government in which the state abolishes private property and takes over industry in the name of the people. Communist regimes have often been modeled on the Soviet Union, which curtailed people's basic freedoms.

General Staff A group of officers, concerned with personnel, equipment, planning, and overall strategy, who assist military commanders in the field.

habeas corpus The constitutional requirement that an arresting officer explain to a judge why a prisoner is being held in custody.

National Guard State military forces whose training and equipment are partially funded by the U.S. Government. Units can be called up to serve in the United States Army in times of crisis.

Leapfrogging A World War II strategy used by Allied forces in the Pacific. Heavily fortified enemy-held islands were bypassed and weaker outposts were captured to build airstrips for the

next advance, thus cutting off Japanese lines of
supply and communication.

Plebe   A first-year cadet at West Point.

Rank insubordination   Deliberately defying orders
from a superior officer. This is a serious and punishable military offense.

Trench warfare   Combat between opponents occu-
pying deep, muddy ditches surrounded by barbed
wire and separated by a "no-man's-land."
Attempts to cross "no-man's-land" generally pro-
duced high casualty rates for a gain of only a few
yards of territory.

A NOTE ON SOURCES

I looked at a number of biographies of Douglas MacArthur, including books written by some of the men who served under him. With so much material on the general, I chose to focus on two relatively recent books: *American Caesar* by William Manchester (New York: Dell, 1978), a somewhat sympathetic account of the general, and *Old Soldiers Never Die* by Geoffrey Perret (Holbrook, Massachusetts: Adams, 1997.) This second book is more critical of the general and contains the most up-to-date research on his life. I also read memoirs by MacArthur himself, *Reminiscences* (New York: McGraw-Hill, 1964), and by Harry Truman, *Year of Decisions* and *Years of Trial and Hope* (New York: Doubleday, 1955–1956). These accounts were less helpful because the authors were often more interested in defending themselves than in presenting the facts accurately.

To get a balanced view of MacArthur's career and to better understand the historical background, I also consulted the following books: Roger Burlingame's *General Billy Mitchell* (New York: Signet Books, 1956),

Kazuo Kawai's *Japan's American Interlude* (Chicago: University of Chicago Press, 1960), Michael Schaller's *The American Occupation of Japan* (New York: Oxford University Press, 1985), James C. Thomson Jr., Peter W. Stanley, and John Curtis Perry's *Sentimental Imperialists* (New York: Harper Torchbooks, 1985), and T. H. Watkins's *The Great Depression* (Boston: Little Brown and Company, 1993).

To better appreciate the general's military successes and failures, I also examined the sections on MacArthur in Henry Steele Commager's *Pocket History of the Second World War* (New York: Pocket Books, 1945), Harry A. Gailey's *The War in the Pacific* (Novato, California; Presidio, 1995), S. L. A. Marshall's *World War I* (Boston: Houghton Mifflin, 1987), Callum A. MacDonald's *Korea* (New York: Free Press, 1986), and Ronald H. Spector's *Eagle Against the Sun* (New York: Viking Press, 1984).

FOR MORE INFORMATION

Feinberg, Barbara Silberdick. *Harry S. Truman.* New York: Franklin Watts, 1994.

Freedman, Russell. *Franklin Delano Roosevelt.* Boston: Houghton Mifflin, 1992.

Lindop, Edmund. *Woodrow Wilson, Franklin Delano Roosevelt, Harry S. Truman.* New York: Twenty-first Century Books, 1995.

McGowen, Tom. *The Korean War.* New York: Franklin Watts, 1992.

———*World War I.* New York: Franklin Watts, 1993.

———*World War II.* New York: Franklin Watts, 1993.

Scott, Robert Alan. *Douglas MacArthur and the Century of War* (Makers of America Series). New York: Facts on File, 1997.

Steel, Philip. *Between the Two World Wars.* Chicago: Silver Burdett, 1994.

INTERNET RESOURCES

http://sties.communitylink.org/mac/
The MacArthur Memorial website, with exhibits, library, and archives.

http:/users.deltanet.com/~cybrgbl/macarthur/do uglas-macarthur-farewell.html The text of MacArthur's farewell speech.

INDEX

Page numbers in *italics* indicate illustrations.

Australia, 11, 71, 73–74, 76
Awards/honors
  DSC, 40, 81
  DSM, 47–48, *47*, 62, 102
  from Japan, 113
  medal of honor, 73
  parade, *108*, 109
  silver star, 40
  Sylvanus Thayer Award,
    114

Baker, Newton D., 37–38,
  39, 42
Blaik, Earl, 76, 112
Bliss, Tasker, *39*
Bonus Army, 58–61, *60*
Brooks, Louise, 51–53, *52*,
  54, 57–58

Chiang Kai-shek, 95–96, 100
China, 11, 32, 66, 95–96, *98*,
  99–105, 107, 109, 111
Chronology, 117–119
Civilian Conservation Corps,
  61–62
Cleveland, Grover, 22
Clothes, 40–42, *41*
Collaborators, 81–82
Communism, 95–96. *See
  also* Korea

Draft, 37–38, 89

Eisenhower, Dwight D., 59,
  65, 78, 85, 111

Faircloth, Jean, 62, 63–64,
  63, 68–69, 76, 80, 85, 107,
  110, 115
Far East tour, 32

France, 11, 37, 38–40, 44–46, *45*, 65

Gibbons, Jean, 80
Grant, Ulysses, 23
Grant, Ulysses S. III, 23, 25

Harding, Warren, *51*
Hardy, Mary Pinkney. *See* MacArthur, Pinky
Hazing, 27–28, 50
Hirohito, 84–88, *86*, *88*
Homma, Masaharu, 90
Hoover, Herbert C., 58, 59, 61
Huerta, Victoriano, 34, 37
Hurley, Patrick, 59, 61

Japan, 32, 65–82, 107, 110, 113, 116
    and communism, 95
    occupation, 83–97, *84*, *86*, *88*
    and Pearl Harbor, 9–10, 67
    surrender, 9–12, *10*, *13*
Johnson, Ladybird, 115
Johnson, Lyndon B., 115

Kennedy, John F., 113
Kenney, George C., 12, 76,77
Korea, 96, 97–107, *98, 106*, 109, 111, 116

Leapfrogging, 77
Lincoln, Abraham, 87

MacArthur, Arthur (brother), 16, 18, *19*, 21–22, 23, 54
MacArthur, Arthur (son), 64, 69, *69*, 76, 80, 85, 106, 115
MacArthur, Arthur, Jr. (father), 17, 18–19, *19*, 22, 23, 25–27, *26*, 32, 33, 90, 91
MacArthur, Douglas, *2*
    birth, 16
    childhood, 17–19, *19*
    death, 114–115
    education, 19–22, *21*
    marriages, 51–53, *52*, 63, *63*
MacArthur, Judge, 22
MacArthur, Malcolm, 16, 18
MacArthur, Mary, 62
MacArthur, Pinky (mother), 16–17, 18, *19*, 20, 22–25, *24*, 28, 30, 31, 34, 42, 49, 53, 54, 58, 62
MacArthur Memorial, 115, *116*
Mann, William, *39*
Mao Zedong, 95
March, Peyton, 43
Marshall, George C., 70, 78
Martin, Joseph, 105
McKinley, William, 22, 27
Medal of Honor, 36, 47, 55, 73
Memoirs, 114
Mexico, 34–37, *35*, 55
Mitchell, Billy, 55–56

Mosely, Philip, 61

Olympics, 56–57, *57*
Osmena, Sergio, 53, *54*, 78, 81
Otjen, Theabold, 22

Pearl Harbor, 9–10, 67
Percival, A.E., *13*
Perry, Matthew, 9
Pershing, John J., 38, 42–43, 46–48, *47*, 53, 55
Personality, 12, 14–15, 115–116
Philippines, 31, 53–54, *54*, 57–58, 62–65, 89, 113–114, 116
  and MacArthur (father), 23, 25, *26*, 27, 90, 91
  WW II, 65–74, *68, 69, 73, 75*, 77–82, *79*
Pierce, Franklin, 18

Quezon, Manuel, 53, *54*, 62, 63, 66, 71

Rainbow (42nd) Division, 37–48, *39, 46, 47*
Rank insubordination, 105
Remington Rand Company, 112
Rhee, Syngman, 89
Ridgway, Matthew P., 106
Roosevelt, Eleanor, 76
Roosevelt, Franklin D., 61, 65–66, 71, 77, 81

Roosevelt, Theodore, 33
Roxas, Manuel, *54*, 81–82

Soviet Union, 65, 95, 96, 97, 101, 103, 109
Sports, 21, *21*, 29, 50, 112

Taft, Robert, 110–111
Taft, William H., 25
Truman, Harry, 81, 82, 89, 96, 99, 100–101, 102, 103, 104, 109
  fires MacArthur, 105–107, *107*
  opinion of MacArthur, 14

United Nations, 97, 99, 105

Vietnam, 113

Wainwright, Jonathan, *13*
Washington, George, 16, 87
Weeks, John, *51*
West Point, 12, 22–25, *24*, 27–30, 49–51, *51*, 53, 114
Wilson, Woodrow, 36, 38
Wood, Leonard, 34, 36
WW I, 37–48, *39, 41, 43, 45, 46, 47*, 49
  Bonus Army, 58–61, *60*
WW II, 9–12, *10*, 13, 65, 67–82, *68, 69, 73, 75, 79*, 95, 97

Yamashita, Tomoyuki, 89–90